WONDERMENTAL

NICO VASSILAKIS ditches deep city for rural, bodegas for cornfields, and subways for hay rakes without any pastoral yearning — rather, these poems reckon with the effects of situation and absorption — pandemic, locale, digital realities, domesticity, place norms and forms of transmission — and wonder at it all. Is it the place, or how we're found to be there?

WONDERMENTAL is questioning and madcap, sober and reflective, delighted, wry, and aghast. Nothing's as tidy as a hay rake or as obvious as a graffiti'd silo. Noise is a certain surround, but self, encompassed, still hopes to extricate mattering: "You will salvage what is erased in / order to read what transpired".

– C Turnbull

©2024 Nico Vassilakis

ISBN 979-8-9902208-5-0

Published by Pulley Press,
an imprint of
Clyde Hill Publishing

Cover and book design by Dan D Shafer

WONDERMENTAL
NICO VASSILAKIS

PULLEY
PRESS

Dedicated to my wife Crystal

A Preface 1

CONTACT: Hurrayentire 3

COMPLYING 7
CAUSALITY REPORT 9
2014.... 12
WHAT TREMENDOUS DISTANCE 13
SWOLLEN NIGHTSTAND 18
WHY DOESNT MATTER ANYMORE: Ladybugs 19
TREE No. 14 20
ONE OCCASION DELIGHTS 22

AFTERNOON GUY IN HADES 26
A PAUSE OR A LAPSE 30

THAT MANNEQUIN AT GIMBELS 34
CLUMPS OF NORMIES 36
I AM YOUR NEW FORMAL 37
FEMALE ARMSTRONG 37
SHAPE AS AN EVENT 39
WE ARE QUADRILATERALS 40
THE MISSHAPEN MEDALLION 41
AS THE CITIZENRY RELOCATES 42
AS INTENSE FOCUS GOES AWRY 44
WALTER CRONKITE 45

SO EQUALS DO 51

   In the Time of Pre Vax 53

   Vertigo in the Grass 54

   Get Over Yourself 55

   The Camper 56

   The Pond 58

   The Ridden Mower 59

   The Shouse 60

   The Chicken Coop 61

   The Forward Exits 62

   The Backyard Hinge 64

   This Silo In Its Resting Position 64

   The Fallen Walnuts 66

   The Sheds 67

   The Fire Pit 67

   The Solar Panels 67

   The Night Sky 69

   The Concrete Slab 69

ENTRUSTED LITTLE PAPERS 75

HOLA PAPELITO 76

About the Poet 85

a preface

WONDERMENTAL is a weave of bliss and turmoil, a found text in nature, leaning against a hot dog stand. It's a film playing on the curve of a silo. This is the way men talk to one another here in the country. *How much water's in the rain gauge? When's your next mow?* The names of things change to the names of things. Corn once, Soy twice, but Wheat's first. Farmers markets, car shows in the parking lot, hayrides through town. **WONDERMENTAL** arises in sections marking the land and its features: the chicken coop, the shed, the pond, and the fallen walnuts.

Inside these collaged writing time spans, **WONDERMENTAL** fuses moments and accumulates fragments. It's a scroll on a phone, a set of interrupted drives from one place to the next, a way to know the land. The exploration crosses perforated boundaries into the hinterland.

WONDERMENTAL entails living through the early rigors of COVID and obsessing over the poison issuing from political theater in the media. All that came after picking up and moving from the Bronx to rural Greenville, IL, some broodish episode of Green Acres. Birdsong, coyotes howling, tornado warnings instead of the honking, bodega vibes, and subway stops of the city. Getting under a new family tree. Resistant to the leaves. Being and getting old all at the same time—

W O N D E R M E N T A L .

CONTACT:
Hurrayentire

Welcome to it. I never thought sentences out my mouth. No
way to be in charge of associations. It's our home. Not even
pictures of the next step.
I feel menaced by nature or
better put—pulverized
         and

COMPLYING

May I step in here
for a second

Her rings were slippery with butter

The unrelenting

Duodenum follies

My personal history with nicotine
addiction

A proposal of prompts designed to
alleviate
The failures we amass
The garbage that accrues

A tincture
A pellet
A squadron of capsules

A heck of a lot of misspellings
throughout the city

That time

When a word broke in half and
letters started bleeding

And now

An hour away from the Mississippi
River

I might be a bookmark for a larger
untold story

Let's not get carried away

CAUSALITY REPORT

Graffiti on silos

Shopping portable radiation
detectors online

I'm getting absorbed
I know it's related to my outlook
But I don't have the strength to stop
feeling absorbed

Holding up a sign that reads
MEANWHILE BACK IN THE BLACK
HOLE

Noise is everywhere

My silences lately
make me think about dementia

Do you prefer a systemic
dismantling or a singular devastating
action?

They saved telecommunication
cable to remember landline phones

———

I am
Dimensioning

It's like glass out there
Not one vibration out of place

The whispers
The taunts

A visual bandwidth of jettisoned letter fragments and receivable material

A god-damn parade

A pile of cheerleaders in distress

And sitting here on a bench by the Dairy Queen with the local paper in my hands

Stumpy
Shakey
Spanky
Swampy
Snipe
Stoney
(Spongee)

alternate names:
Slumpy
Smudge
Smidge
Sonar

All receivable materials

Hello sirs

The time for extinguishing
is approaching

The sonic accumulation of things

The holy vestibule

A palimpsest of miniature
happenstance

Promenade down funky Broadway
till the cows come home, my friend

We have finally pierced the
circumference of the situation

2014...

I forgot my phone at home today. That was okay, liberating, revealing how I create and occupy my own down-time with phone use. While on the subway I wanted to know the time and I wasn't on one of the lines that displays the time. I was tempted to look at the person across from me and do what I usually do—point at my wrist while asking, what time do you have? I realized that the person across from me might not know what that gesture meant as they were glued to their phone. The phone has the time, but what gesture does one create to go about asking for the time?

WHAT TREMENDOUS DISTANCE

To sit in languid repose

A potential of accumulated

Possibilities

In conclusion we discussed

Letters from your birthday

Lettuce from my bandmates

Growerier and Growerier

This room befits

You are as old as the harvests you've seen

Or a hawk bouncing off the windshield

Or machete season in a fabricated landscape

Or panic thunder radio

This room befits it

―――

One can sing
The other can't do nothing

I don't trust the one that can't do
nothing

Esther Williams
Ethel Merman
Harmon Killebrew
What's it matter

How is it I've grown fatigued
of my own imagination

Blasphemy is mostly laziness
in this part of town

A torrent
A wave
An inability to encapsulate
the future

We know nothing

―――

Something happened
last night

We built a cloud

―――

I wear you like a mood

I mistook the rose for a woodpecker

On this day
The world can end
anytime

And you insist new economic theories
are required for the planet to survive

Yes, I can be oblivious to your feelings
and for that I apologize

You are my sunshine
my ONLY currency

The quiet of an image is broken

A man inside a hatless nap

Speaking through letters

How many birds does it take to kill a frog?

The story of the usual you
starts with matriarchy
because women are magic
till the boys suppress that
so completely it becomes patriarchy

It's like making Christmas albums all year round

Now I don't believe in anything

Well, anything

———

He entered the ring and actually
began to box

A heckler's veto

A sugared stance of power

How many times does it come
around again
This

I wear you like melancholy

Cups of laughing milk everywhere

I keep going to the well
but I need to become the well

———

Nearby is where I find you
Inside DNA

A raft of trinkets
made to resemble a scene
We relive
over and over

Again we wind up
in a pile of gestures
Saying more than words
can possibly

So that stopping
becomes the goal

SWOLLEN NIGHTSTAND

Just a few priests sitting around getting
drunk—you know, high-end booze and
cigars

And the tears that I cried for that
woman are gonna fuck you big river
And I'm gonna sit right here till I die

What is it for text to visually encompass
itself. What is a poem but a
sum of its parts on display

Allegheny Moon
Fly Me to the Moon
Moonage Daydream
Bad Moon Rising
Harvest Moon
The Killing Moon
Walking on the Moon
Pink Moon
Moonshadow
Moonlight Mile
Moonlight Drive
Blue Moon of Kentucky
Half Moon
Dead Moon

And so on

No pocket no pocket

WHY DOESNT MATTER ANYMORE:
Ladybugs

This year has been the worst as far as ladybugs amassing in corners, on the sills, crawling across the ceiling, the floor, the walls. Hundreds and hundreds of ladybugs vacuumed. Yet still they come, drop down in front of you or onto your neck or strolling over a napkin, your shoe, the sink. Everywhere really.

TREE No. 14

The chugging sound in the distance
is having its way with my ears
Wanting to locate a source
The contortion with less wobble

Schedule A
So o
So o. O
So o oooo oO
Underwater terrorism
and from here

A rabbit snare

Labrum tears

Chocolate ice cream soda

"—pray the divine powers that be to
ease the insufferability and pain that
endlessly lessens the fleshed xerox of
God."
      from *The Golden Dot*, Gregory Corso

"Now that we have no need to do
anything
What shall we do?"
      from "Untitled Anarchist Poem", John Cage

Sits here
Thinking about inflight entertainment
How Mylar over Mylar
makes a movable image
makes a classroom a playfield

Purports to be a revolution in turn
The volume dial gets all melty in my
hand

Things are hyper focused and very
singular. It comes down to wielding
monoculars, sticks of vision.
The greater good is less and less of a
concern to our diminished population
and that makes 'em nervous

This poem, this act of fragmented
writing, isn't located anywhere
particular, but here within itself

*...a time to embrace, and a time to
be far from embraces*

ONE OCCASION DELIGHTS

Be translucent with me

All the Muybridge animals
leaving the ground at the same time

Nothing I'm saying
will linger long enough to change
your way of thinking

So, why be here?

Here's why

The end

AFTERNOON GUY IN HADES

The 714 Quaalude and Beatlemania

The symphony dragged on
Three spotted horses along the fence

How we negotiate space

The past is not a competition
it just adds up

Something about
telling you how I feel
so well that you recognize it
as your own response

Yes, up and down the hallway
with its head leaking

Said, you're blocking the sound I make
with the sound I make

Some minor mischief
tucked away in advance of itself

No one chooses to live like this
but we end up this way

Embarrassed by it

Unprepared to slip into nothingness
like this awkward poem

———

Rosie, I didn't know you were a flower
when I first laid eyes on you

Then you fell from the trees gigantic
and landed next to me right here on the
couch

―――

Eh,
Mouth riddler?

Down by the river

People collect words in
predictable ways

When I listen
I know what you're going to say

Down by the beach

A concentric circus of what's
Imminent
Critical
Important
Routine

―――

This is how it ends up...
Anticipatory negativity

May the bird of paradise fly up your
nose

That thing's happening again
where Orion's Belt is hanging low
at the end of our driveway

He mused about how to re-donut the
entire idea

———

I am all the time

You don't have to go home, but you
can't stay here

Take from the dormant pile

Imp
Imply

The museum of raised eyebrows

Once again
There I was
Randomly watching
A movie on an app
And the door opens
And there you are
And I'm like
What!
What the fuck dude!
There you are
Again
You
Again
On a screen

Hey! Captain's hat!

A prize
inside the pencil

It's just you
shadowboxing at noon

―――

Was it a pasture, a field, a prairie,
a forest, timber, a meadow

Somewhere on the timeline
tinkers with trajectory

Gussied up with thoughts
A revolution of outerwear

I'm here long enough to be here for a
reason

All the subject matter has left me

A PAUSE OR A LAPSE

Why carry a tedious mirror?

I am inside the citadel

A bulbous radio
inside this fast mouth

Anyone goes anywhere
Fingers follow tassels

From the bodega to corn fields
Environments shed their viral loads

I am still with you

WOMEN

NDER
ITAL

THAI MANNEQUIN AT GIMBELS

They asked, what is this music?
Oh, it's the go-to-hell boogie

As words become more meaningless

My tongue actually starts bleeding

He barricaded himself in the chicken coop

Altogether dancing to the smoke
of an unattended cigarette

An extraction, he said, was required
by midweek

This was a definite threat

More so than a kaleidoscope on acid

I can't make out what these letters
are saying

These drawn lines parading around

A row of pistols in holsters

Full of potential

And here I remain the only masked
hombre on the plane

You know what? is not the best
conversation starter

What do you think of that shit? is
sort of better kindling

A fire pit
A tonsillectomy
A hedgehog
A muffler
I don't know how to stop

CLUMPS OF NORMIES

A radar indicated threat
Tornado debris

Sure, let the world transcribe you

Our time here is intense and short

In a state of barefooted resolve

I once thought I was something then I became something else

Pliable

Like sculpture

Available to manipulation

Where you end up is inconsequential

Destination's always been a farce

Tracing forms
Climbing trees
Gazing upon and away from yourself

It's the action that transmits

It's the indicator

The rest is mere holding pattern

I AM YOUR NEW FORMAL FEMALE ARMSTRONG

Something shook out her kerchief

From the vertical to the coaxial
From the ventricle to the horizontal

Echolocate the grid
Quash the threads
Squealing through joy

What's this going in at one end
and coming out the other

The library across the street is
burning up her walls

Lampposts with bodies taped
to them

This town has said all it's going
to say

As the scribblers are digitized
the originals are being thrown out

You stand in front of a mirror
dressed in a lavish array of
festoonery and all you'll see
is asymmetry

A squeaky frog in a palace of
motherboards

That remnant of a differing time

A certain poker hand

Reliable, dependable

A cornerstone of the community

Gewgaws of immense power

A bogus god exploiting your psychic energy

Touchéd

SHAPE AS AN EVENT

You're so lost up your ass in
New York grooviness that you
don't know what's real

Movies on silos
And ribbons through forests
Day after day glows
And jumping off towers

Wherever it is there's something there

There's something out there in
space talkin' 'bout my generation

The whole hand-holding love thing
with everybody has gone to shit

This human condition won't
stop ruining lives
stop getting us killed
stop taking over the conversation

You should be overzealous about
something
Well, fuck that

I don't know where it goes from here

It's a failure in programming

WE ARE QUADRILATERALS

We're all regular people

A raucous blend and clear thumping ambition

Disdain for the other was the thing that broke us

There's nothing left to discuss

By that I mean a lack of originality

I've been sniffing around a variety of templates to accommodate all the shitty ideas we amass

And there ain't nothing new yet

Bejeweled apathy

Preferring to live in virtual life

A slave to technology

Rotten economic theories

You can say we're fucked

And you'd be right

THE MISSHAPEN MEDALLION

The lavender bells
When the hawks hop back
I enter this small town
I mean it's small
A post office and a beer store
Making North American room
Space enough to activate
the hardier portions of a sentence
that keep the conversation moving
There are these shapes out there
that go unattended
And as a nicety
I try to find common ground or have
only your interests
brought up

To the earthling there...
Your planet is a refreshing stop
on such a longer way to go

I accumulate information

I'm nearly an asshole or I'm simply
ignored

Sound in an enclosed place is best

AS THE CITIZENRY RELOCATES

I see more here like peripherally

I draw (my kite)

There's a bastion of clues that await
your attention

Kincaid, Bulpitt, and Tovey
and then straight through to Decatur
and we'll see a duke in Decatur

I'm a duke and you're a duck
I don't wanna be a duck
and I don't want you to be a duke
I know what a dog is
but I don't know what a duke is
You're not a duke
You're a handsome man
No, you're a pretty lady

A pair of sunflowers, he thought,
with middles staring their way into
the far end of an ashtray. Nothing
comes out right here. These winged
things breathing all around us. A
rhythm that keeps the chairs moving

The ship was sinking. The lifeboats
released. Due to crowding and
fervent ideologies, the truth
never made it on and was left to live
underwater, out of reach, not in our
presence

But who's creating a dynamic retail landscape for these kids to shop in?

AS INTENSE FOCUS GOES AWRY

The side jab, a side job, a real meal
I love my wife, that is truer and truer
There's nowhere to go
A light will fall upon you, will cleanse
you
My god's a space alien, a hall
monitor roaming the galaxy
Sometimes I can be insanely
efficient
Otherwise malarkey
Contraband
Arugula
Need I add defenestrate
Please
I said, I love my wife
That is enough
The chaos stops here
No, here
I mean, here

WALTER CRONKITE

There it is
I fell out of bed

Okay, so
Let's call it hygiene theatre
or early COVID

She said, "I'm confused and I think
I'm going to hell"

Cranium, space, indigenous
rhododendron, a soft crevice to
exhale into or thrift store puzzles

A valentine cupcake with pink frosting
I describe it as metal tongue

Even the symbolic stuff won't help
here

A combine of creativity
An afghan of thin anxiety
A vintage drinking bird pecks
on the kitchen counter

I'll conjure my second mind to
attention

And now they're coming to kill you

There is no soothing your heart
when it's torn apart
by the news of the world

Poetry is a jive turkey in this scenario

All your handheld devices getting
soaked in a pool of information porn

The accurate and the inaccurate
Somewhere beyond what's breathable

It's too painful to edit anymore

WONDER

MENTAL

SO EQUALS DO

I sacrifice my place in line for being
somewhere else

Oh climate, oh disregard

While walking out the timber naked
and scratched

Even my own bird laughs

This is what it looks like at this time
of day when a sunbeam hits our
overhead light spraying the room
with prism fragments

It's a classic distribution of wealth
where you're stabbed in the eye and
kicked down the stairs at the same time

It's turbines, it's dials, it's clocks
you wear on your wrist

The whole of futurity is pausing at
what happens next

Self-promotion disguised as altruism
is still self-promotion, so don't add
flowers to make it smell better

Having gone, I'll tell you there's
nothing like finding yourself lost
in a place you don't quite know how you
got there

A little schmear of domentia cream

Enter sleep
In the usual way
Squeezing between
The letters
Of the word
To get through
To the other side

It's so hot out, you submerge into
water

So, I do

From one environment into another

She said: *I'm selling my pork chops
but I'm givin' my gravy away*

She asked: *Does your money fold
or does it jingle*

He ate Blast Simply, little candies
from a bag, and watched the
volcano erupt across the street

It's time again to make an alphabet
out of twigs

A bolt of Thursday filled the sky

This board game is damn warped

I can talk the way tendrils emerge
and assume other speaking avenues
of thought, but today is a spicy end

In the Time of Pre Vax

The situation is about losing your
past by growing out of it. The
unbending vestige is an ugly thing

Yet you can't escape behind you

I missed a few possible entries into
the conversation, and so I started
internalizing my thoughts

The fecal reach of everything

Any tranquility you find here will be
temporary

Now that writing has ended there's
not much to say

I'll tell you a little about how it's
been, but i won't really tell you how
it's going

Your enemies love certain things

Typewritten instructions on index
cards

Oatmeal farina cream of wheat

Something's run afoul

I lost all my computer files

There is no poetry, no eloquence
to save us from ourselves

There is no
And it's been
Did you read that
Across the nation
Quality control is
One depression isn't
A boat was spotted
A concert of bullfrogs
Retaliation was required
The use of tongs
The light was so
A targeted group

Vertigo in the Grass

A weather wheel of sorts
There's a distinction
Paradise waits
Theories abound
The clouds came rushing
I know several really
The moon is not
Won't you consider
The screens melted away
We hugged just before
Let's place those out by
If there's a flat
The bee is an afternoon

I was devoid of
The quarantine was
Two holes in the dingy

There is no jockeying for position.
The trees most exposed to light
survive

The subway, the underground
thrives with its scurrying and active
subconscious

Noise is the brick and mortar

A sea without eyes, six without nine
or know without seeing

It's all a knot, the pleasure of fitting

It's been two days
It's been three weeks
It's been four and a half months
since

Get Over Yourself

The bodies suffocate from
a lack of oxygen

We keep living through history like
it's intentional

Over and over again the winner is
kept aloft by the loser's scaffold

The fingers work for the palm as the
palm works for the wrist

I'll tell you this, you will continue
even with your crashed hard drive

Spring is the most fecund, how it
dresses trees with leaves every time

The subtle out in the open, out in
the middle of nowhere. An
odd conjunction with nature. The
rhetorics of how am I supposed to
make myself heard

The Camper

What can I tell you about being
adjacent to an endless gaping void

The diorama has no light fixtures
and is not quite yet a livable space

Forget about the concrete

Forget about the mythological
figures

Drag racing with blinders on. The
nothing imbued with specialness

Seems I don't care anymore

I lost my way
I can't fashion lush poesy on a dare
I'm all thumbs

Abandoned business districts after
rush hour

"Tents of nomads frozen into stone"
Arendt

A collapsible view tucked like
thoughts fold into cloud

Tumult is killing me. Thrashing
through the snowbound Charlies
all revved up and squawking

I could hold my tongue down on the
t in tungsten long enough to run amok
in the grapple part of a shade tree

Yes, I hummed my way through
a breathalyzer

TTTTTTTTTTT

The sweet mucus of revenge
sloganeering its way down
the benefactor's throat

Someone's being coerced,
you can smell it.
Maybe it's me

My anxiety is ordinary.
It stems from attempts at initiating
organizational ideas
that never get started

Time for psilocybin

This is my heel

Defunct as a musical score

The Pond

This is a containment zone

You go somewhere, you become
part of the economy

We need more candles for the
power outage

People are strange, even on
a playground they'll vie for dominance

There's something delusional
about reaching for sweets

Options designed to kill specific
nerve endings

You'll have to throttle the garment
to release the microbes

You'll have to fashion a satisfactory
response to these inevitable
questions

Differing postures attract a variety
of potential endorsements

Eating crackers while talking

There won't be an easier time than
now

The Ridden Mower

Which is to say, I hate lists

One calamity, two Janes, three
High-stake points of view and
four pass cards

I gotta have those pass cards

I was whatchamacallit

I was Breeze

I was given the name of my super
hero power, The Mingler

It's an inflammatory set of questions,
a survey conducted in conflict

Whatever. It forks

I sense deviation, a ripple at the
central intake valve of this poem

Is it food or a relationship

It's the exchange of money, really

I'll throw chiaroscuro in just for
contrast. The difference between
authority and power

Keeps us subservient and giddy with
a bag of treats

Ruination is charming as a cleanser

Totally lazy
Totally wired

The glowing orange ember before
the toast pops up

I can't help you.
And even if I could
this lane is closed

The Shouse

It's a machine with an LED display
that announces death

It's fine, these units come with
an internal weeping system

From a distance I explain in the
least amount of syllables

Gwa Vong Koo Ehrtey Sheemza

You'll need a pick axe, a spade
and a post hole digger
to finish the trench

Those are the basic instructions

It's like someone in the family
winning the lottery

We all feel good

The protesters are holding up
blank signs, but they're
still getting arrested

Doesn't matter what you say, but
where you say it, I guess

The Chicken Coop

What is torn remains

To circle a word, to keep focused upon
it

There are fewer exits than
there are ways to enter

An object that holds writing

Even your grittonage faithfully
recounts the event

You will salvage what is erased in
order to read what transpired

Being free is not easy
Society involves entrapment

You know, I can't be in charge of
myself

It might seem interesting, but not
enough to take the extra steps required

This shit is unrelenting.
Caught in loops you can't shake

We are weak. Our beauty is in being frail

They provide the tension, but we
pull back before we break

The advertisements are the show.
Everything else is just there to keep
you glued to the screen

The Forward Exits

Where you and decay and death
sit in a happy hand-holding family
circle without insurance

The crumpled images, the anti-psychotic,
the burned edges,
the title itself—

In your absence

The redemptive
Acquisition
of
Cheerful
Disposition

Now that's trying

Lie down, dear, Lie down

My feeling about that is
there will be a kind of new
perfection achieved

As to the future getting absorbed
How circumference kills
Keeps intuition awake
Keeping an eye out for signs

The alignment between what I'm
not thinking and what I'm not saying
is making itself known

Therein is a high bar, an
entanglement of bebopdom at just
the right portions

As if this sentence hasn't lost its
baby fat

It's like I'm sleeping for two people
Black white and green

Was always uptight about how
I was going to get home

The Backyard Hinge

There is this thing and it's
Valium in the parking lot

You associate the future with some
direction

Truth and finances

Left hand smoke

In the middle of dense text you will
see the word saccade

The wonderment of things gets
fucked up
I've got a back-up heat lamp for just
this situation

This Silo In Its Resting Position

It's select, it's select all, or it's paste

The kind of devoted voter willing
to put it on the line

Some text in need of juggling

Okay, so, I outsourced some of my
small talk in order to focus on the
greater invisible and how we tinker
with minutia

There's hamburger and hamburger
helper

The shoreline is the easiest demarcation,
she said, to negotiate
between heaven and hell

It's an owner's manual

I've mentioned that before

The new economy is soon upon us.
The one where people go missing
not just from age and disease, but
from something much more
deliberate

Yes, reach out and touch a friend

Call them

By their names

your grasp at fumes will despoil
what's left of earthly meaning

On the top shelf there, you will find
reams of paper filled with ideas on
how to leave the planet

Aggressive musical chairs

Bruising

and Darwin

Lifting the tone arm off the album

There's something about looking up
at the sky and floating away forever

The Fallen Walnuts

Rough air, Con Air, derrière, Buenos Aires

A stutter and the struggle to imbibe
regular air

Free air

I will keep you close to the vest

Will make a nest of shredded tires
off the interstate

The kind of radio dial
that tunes in the finery,
the accidental static of divination

The spiky racket of broadband
raised from a corpse

A ribbed xylophone

And I'll live in this tree

Alongside the brick walls of the
canyon with its whirlpools of trash

Said garbage

The Sheds

I love annihilation

I will remove your implanted
temporal surveillance

The cats will all be out of the bag

From here on out, I'll let my shoe
trees do all the walking

Built on the backs of the working
class, this new place is too showy
with no substance

All in all, I'm done

The Fire Pit

A certain red timeline
Will nudge sparklers
To stare at a hard verb

Coyotes, coyotes
The ace passes a bottle around
Even dogs snore perfect smoke rings

The Solar Panels

You let your hands move over flame

The cliché of you finding yourself
caught in a long hallway of doors

A child's head too close to the
radiating source

The conspiracy

A handful of coins and rocks

I'll check again, but am pretty sure
weather will always be there

Cozy up to fame, so warm and
destitute

Pieces of bloodied gauze return
as bookmarks to previous readings

The shape of a funnel too will
attract your thoughts

What an excellent feature these eyes

These fiery pupils that follow the
elaborates

Even associative jargon finds its way
to a bullseye

We're friends marked by the journey

That sound behind where we are
now

Making itself known

The Night Sky

These are the times you forget

God has gotten smaller

Gold inscribed surprise right there

Where the eyes jack into the brain

Something rare acquires value
only to the seller

Or a bag of chips that offers more
chips than the bag can handle

Oh my

This bird stayed up all night telling
us its troubles

And yes, the algorithms gather
more useful results for business than
for the people

Pfft! That's how movies always start.

The Concrete Slab

When there's nothing to say or do

Up a heavenly path

Thistle bags filled for the birds

I won't even fasten my seat belt
this time around

A tremendous strain is upon us
The monkey grinder lives outside my pocket

Yes, I'm smiling behind my mask

Can you guess what's been happening?

Come on, guess

WONDER

MENTAL

ENTRUSTED LITTLE PAPERS

Stairway stairway, starlight

Left you for dead
when I left

Little paper notes from the Bronx

HOLA PAPELITO

"Charting relationships in language"
I lifted that line
My object relationship
A letter
collapses into a word
"We're building a machine
that'll be more
sensitive"
I lifted that line
The buoyancy punctured
Sentences only slightly
different from each other
"Are you remembering for me"
I lifted that as well
A line goes for a walk
walks through the house
What is it to make
a beautiful thing

―――

Candy on your doorstep, on
your desktop

This time it's different, I want to
destroy you

―――

You tell me what's important...
environment is, to me, an instant classic.
I want so much for you to love me...
but
an accumulation of energy gets exhausted

Very honored to be included...
Considered legitimate for half the country
It's pieces of a puzzle torn from my face...
You need to be in therapy, young man
This wave-of-life-coming-toward-you
board game requires one of
the players to be immersed in the void
This weakness lasts just long
enough to produce this:

Cafe Du Monde
Bert Weedon
corpus callosum
lacks of cohesion and a fizzing out

I noticed your post the other day...
for death and forgetting my phone
was awake
yes, for death and forgetting my
phone was awake
I was distracted by another moment
How to not disrupt the building
How to live honestly
Conversation has become shorter
and shorter
What's the crux of what I'm looking
for
I just don't feel committed
The window's a shortcut, but I can't
get it in

———

I'll tell you what I think about last
night in the most basic way I can

Going to bed is too formal

I am oh if
The whole day long
It feels wrong
Someone's taken my whistle away
Yea, it's hitting me alright

This weakness lasts just long
enough to produce this

If I could, I'd wheel you home in that
radio flyer, and no one imagines
being two gigaseconds old

Altar boy ice cream fasting
Spinning across the floor
Tearing off red long johns in the
shower
Moon rocks made of dry dog shit
Low flying meteor
Welcome to the Machine the first
time
Crow flying across the windshield
Decorative kale
Hermit crab on my tongue
Orange orb (Goodbye, Mrs. Ogden)
The space between the STOP and
DO NOT ENTER traffic signs of a
one way street
FM radio and the "Won't Get Fooled Again"
synthesizer solo

Not thinking in words till 15 yrs old
Point, the cat, in my pocket
The dream tree in Inwood Park
Tripping at the produce section with
my dad

———

Olive Oyl

You gotta tie her legs in knots to
make knees

———

The Old Testament
The kingdom of god
The year of the cat
Al Stewart is an astronaut

That's sexy knowledge

———

Mr. Random eyes a sequence
of lived-through events

The way you are expected to be
overworked for the same pay and
smile at the opportunity

There's a station ahead stocked
full with exploration and new devices

External threats are mounting. The
citizenry sense tension and are
willing to take on risk

Rife with intentions. You hear me?

Well, we're a few steps past that

———

It's hard to imagine the blackboard being erased and clown drawings assaulting us for the next few years

This is our status—viral and empty. A propaganda you can trust to fuck you up

———

A twenty-something year old...
I WAS LOOKING TO DOCUMENT WHAT MY LSD EXPERIENCES WERE DOING TO MY BRAIN

It signaled myriad possible manifestos. Insects roaming over the face. Javelins through eyelets, Javelinas through pockets of space. An arabesque throwing you off the double-helix

An armed Ear MD companion dreams of the madre

Grasping for the untranslatables like magnets to a fridge

———

You take up space, it's yours

W O N D E R

M E N T A L

about the poet

NICO VASSILAKIS is a poet and visual artist who drives long distances from his home in rural Illinois where he works as a home healthcare therapist. His clients include farmers, coal workers, truck drivers, accountants, and bank clerks who are recovering from injuries and health issues.

As a poet and artist, Nico Vassilakis has published ten books of poetry and text art. His work explores the unmooring of letters from their word position to create new meanings visually, and in reading. Vassilakis's recent books include *Voir Dire* (Dusie Press 2020) and *Letters of Intent* (CyberWit 2022) along with other pamphlets and booklets. Nico is a contributing editor for UTSANGA, the Italian online magazine of visual language. Nico also coedited *The Last Vispo Anthology: Visual Poetry 1998 – 2008* (Fantagraphics Books 2012) and has curated several international visual/concrete poetry exhibitions. His own visual poetry has been exhibited in shows in Brazil, Russia, Mexico, Germany, Argentina, Canada, and around the US. He cofounded and cocurated the Subtext reading series in Seattle for fifteen years.

WONDERMENTAL traces four years of his new life in the hinterland.

www.ingramcontent.com/pod-product-compliance
Lightning Source LLC
Chambersburg PA
CBHW020212090426
42734CB00008B/1042